MW00783144

Table Decorations with Fruits and Vegetables

Other Schiffer Books on Related Subjects:

Food Art: Garnishing Made Easy, 0-7643-1960-4, $19.95

The Art of Food Sculpture, 0-7643-1454-8, $19.95

Edible Art: Tricks & Tools for Master Centerpieces, 0-7643-2513-2, $19.95

Translated from the German by Dr. Edward Force.

Originally published as *Tischdekorationen Aus Obst und Gemüse zum Selbermachen* by Heel Verlag.

Copyright © 2010 by Schiffer Publishing, Ltd.

Library of Congress Control Number: 2009943716

Photos: Helge Pohl, Bergisch Gladbach
Graphics: Maurizio Pennucci, enowa Deutschland GmbH
Type set in Zurich BT

ISBN: 978-0-7643-3510-5
Printed in China

Published by Schiffer Publishing, Ltd.
4880 Lower Valley Road
Atglen, PA 19310
Phone: (610) 593-1777; Fax: (610) 593-2002
E-mail: Info@schifferbooks.com

For our complete selection of fine books on this and related subjects, please visit our website at **www.schifferbooks.com**.
You may also write for a free catalog.

This book may be purchased from the publisher. Please try your bookstore first.

We are always looking for people to write books on new and related subjects. If you have an idea for a book, please contact us at proposals@schifferbooks.com.

Schiffer Publishing's titles are available at special discounts for bulk purchases for sales promotions or premiums. Special editions, including personalized covers, corporate imprints, and excerpts can be created in large quantities for special needs. For more information, contact the publisher.

Acknowledgements

We would like to thank our photographer, Mr. Helge Pohl, for his ideas, creativity, and his lovely pictures. It was an extremely exciting partnership.

We would also like to thank Christine and Peter Kelch, managers of Hill Metall-waren GmbH, for developing new, high-quality cutting tools and for helping with the ideas that led to this book.

Contents

01

02

Foreword

The art of fruit and vegetable carving has its roots in Asia, but today, creating filigreed edible decorative objects is becoming more and more popular worldwide. No longer is this art form just for professional chefs. Now home cooks are amazing their guests with remarkable, creative decorations for the table and plate.

Unlike the traditional decorations used in the art of cooking, which must be made very laboriously from ingredients like sugar, chocolate, or marzipan, carving fruits and vegetables is relatively easy to learn. You only need to know a few cuts to make a little work of art, and carving fruits and vegetables does not require much time, materials, or tools.

Carved fruits and vegetables, whether in the form of hand carved flowers or a melon rind fruit bowl, give every table a pleasant, fresh atmosphere. Throughout the year you can use seasonal fruits and vegetables to carve figures for a variety of occasions.

Regardless of whether you are a professional chef or a home cook, anyone who likes to decorate with food can use this book to learn how to make attractive decorations for plates, tables, and buffets.

We hope this book will inspire you and awaken your creativity. Perhaps decorating with fruits and vegetables will become your newest hobby.

With step-by-step instructions and numerous tips, we aim to make the beginning carver's first steps as simple as possible. The book provides basic knowledge of various techniques, including how to make simple flowers, figures, and small decorations for plates and glasses. There is also a section of the book that focuses on carving melon and squash motifs. Finally, we complete this introduction to the art of fruit and vegetable carving with detailed instructions on creating small works of art for various seasonal occasions.

Angkana Neumayer

Angkana Neumayer is from Thailand, where she studied fruit and vegetable carving with several renowned carvers. Thanks to her natural talent, carving has become far more than a hobby for her.

Alex Neumayer

Alex Neumayer worked as a chef for seven years in some of Thailand's five-star hotels, including the Central Plaza Hotel in Bangkok and The Westin in Chiang Mai. His artistic interests go back to his younger days when he painted, sculpted, and carved in various media, including fruits and vegetables.

Angkana and Alex Neumayer operate the firm Kochen & Kunst (Cooking & Art), which provides several types of food-related services, including instruction, catering, and consulting. For more information, visit www.kochenundkunst.at.

Angkana and Alex Neumayer have participated in numerous international cooking competitions and have won many awards. Among their greatest successes are winning the Olympiade der Koeche three times and the Culinary World Cup twice.

01 Introduction

Table Decorations with Fruits and Vegetables

Originally, the art of carving fruits and vegetables comes from the Far East. Decorative figures made of fruits and vegetables were carved by hand in China more than a thousand years ago. From there the tradition spread to other Asian cultures. Today, carvings by Chinese and Thai artists are highly valued throughout the world because of their fine, detailed workmanship.

Naturally, fruit and vegetable carving techniques and styles are different in every country. In China, figurative objects, such as animals, ornaments, or human figures, are popular carvings. The Chinese typically use a set of differently shaped and sized carving knives in addition to a standard vegetable knife.

The Thais are the masters of delicate carving. Favorite motifs there are flowers and blossoms made of vegetables, but also a variety of fruits. In the carving tradition of Thailand, only a single knife, or Thai knife is used.

The art of Thai carving is very time-consuming and challenging. Therefore, this introduction to carving is focused on motifs that can be created with Chinese carving knives. With these techniques, the most wonderful objects can be conjured up relatively quickly.

In addition to knives, there are also various patterned cutters that work quickly and allow you to create large quantities of decorative objects in a short time.

Shopping for Fruits, Vegetables, and Tools

To get the most out of carving fruits and vegetables, there are two questions that you should keep in mind from the very beginning:

1. What fruits and vegetables should I work with?
2. What carving tools are the most suitable for what I want to do?

Vegetables and fruits should be fresh and firm, shapely, and free of dents. With melons, mangos, and papayas in particular, you must make sure that the fruits are as unripe as possible. The firmer and fresher the fruit, the simpler it is to carve—and the longer it stays fresh.

Suitable Vegetables

Choose vegetables that are good and firm. Do not use spongy vegetables or those that discolor quickly, such as potatoes. Ideal vegetables for carving are pumpkins, squash, kohlrabi, carrots, radishes, zucchini, beets, etc.

Suitable Fruits

You can actually use any fruits that are firm and not too fibrous. All kinds of melons, mangos, papayas, firm nectarines, and peaches are suitable. Of course you can also use apples and pears, but these fruits do not last long and discolor quickly. Even if they are treated with acid, they usually do not last longer than one day.

How do you Store Your Works of Art?

Put carved vegetables in a container of cold water right after carving. Some types, such as radishes or kohlrabi, can be kept in cold water in the refrigerator for days. Change the water every day. Vegetables that quickly become soft or mushy, such as pumpkin or zucchini, are best wrapped in plastic wrap or placed in a closed container with damp paper towels.

Wrap fruits, except apples and pears, in plastic wrap after carving and store in a cool place. Apples and pears require an acid bath (lemon juice and water), but you can also purchase an acid spray from some specialty shops that carry fruit and vegetable carving supplies.

If you want to decorate buffets or tables with carved fruits and vegetables, you should moisten the objects every half hour with a spray bottle to prevent them from drying out. If you put the carved works of art in cold water in the refrigerator immediately after making them, they will look freshly carved the next morning.

Fruits should be sprayed well again and wrapped in plastic wrap before going into the refrigerator. Using this method, even melons can be used for up to four days.

Not For Eternity

As long as you use really fresh, firm fruits and vegetables, you can keep the carved decorations fresh for a long time.

Carved pumpkins that are properly cooled can remain usable for up to two weeks. Kohlrabi, radishes, and carrots can be preserved for a week. Honeydews and watermelons generally keep their form for up to a week, but muskmelons will not last quite that long. Mangos and ripe papayas will only stay fresh for a few days.

Useful Aids

The following utensils should be readily available when you start carving:

- Cutting board
- One container of cold water (for carved vegetables)
- Scrap container
- Plastic wrap (for carved fruit)
- Kitchen or vegetable knives
- One vegetable peeler (so the unused pieces can be used for cooking)
- Toothpicks or wooden skewers
- One melon spoon (to cut out whole pumpkins or melons)
- Utensils for decoration
- Patterned cutters of your choice
- Cutting tools (Thai knife and carving knife set with whetstone)
- Vegetable adhesive (available in specialty shops)

The Right Cutting Tools

Nowadays a wide variety of tools for decorating and carving are available. Most of these products come from Asia, but some European companies are now making carving sets. As with all kitchen utensils there is a range of quality among these products. Low-priced tools often lack quality, which can make carving difficult.

Only you can decide which carving knife set and decorating tools will be the best for you. Likewise, only you can decide whether to use corers or knives only. To help make these decisions, first consider what you would like to carve—small vegetable objects or whole melons and pumpkins? Only when this question is answered can you select the proper tools and carving set for your work.

The Right Tool for the Job

Only with suitable, sharp tools is carving fruits and vegetables fun and successful. But be careful, when you work with sharp tools the risk of cutting yourself increases. When you purchase your tools, look for sharp, backbone-free blades, which can cut fruits and vegetables but reduces the risk of injury to the user. Cutting with these tools should be smooth because the backs of the blades are not sharp.

The quality of carving knives is seen in their stability. To be sure that the knives keep their shape and stay sharp as long as possible, the functioning parts should be made of hardened steel. Equally important, your tools should be stain and rust resistant since they will have regular contact with aggressive acids.

Nowadays there are many carving knife sets that contain differently shaped blades in several sizes. The more **special knives** you have in your set, the more creative you can be, allowing you to make interesting flowers, figures, and sculptures. By using a variety of blade shapes you can create interesting effects.

Kerf knives cut round or pointed notches in vegetables easily and evenly.

With additional decorating tools, like **ball shapers** in different sizes or **spiral cutters,** you can create interesting effects.

Carrots, radishes, pumpkins, and kohlrabi are firm vegetables that require a certain amount of force. A stable, non-sliding handle makes guiding the knife easier and allows for more precise work. It gives the user a firm grip and thus decreases the danger of injury. Be sure to hold the carving knife properly and always cut away from your body.

The traditional **Thai knife** has one blade. We, however, work with the newly developed **Thai knife**, which has two blades. The symmetrically pointed blade is slightly flexible and sharp on one side. It is used for the fine cuts in Thai carving patterns. The second blade is hollow-ground on one side and is particularly suitable for curved lines and figurative aspects.

Always purchase a **whetstone** that matches the carving set you purchase—it is designed by the manufacturer to match the shapes of the individual carving knives. When sharpening, the whetstone should fit perfectly with how each of the knives cuts.

Working with **pattern cutters** save a great deal of time. You can quickly create considerable quantities of carved object in no time at all. Cut out a section of fruit or vegetable that is about 1 cm thick to determine the basic form of the object. Then, with the carving knives, carve edges and details. Soon the finished object will appear as though it were hand carved.

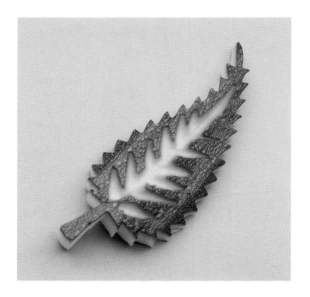

The following page shows the tools we will use in this book.

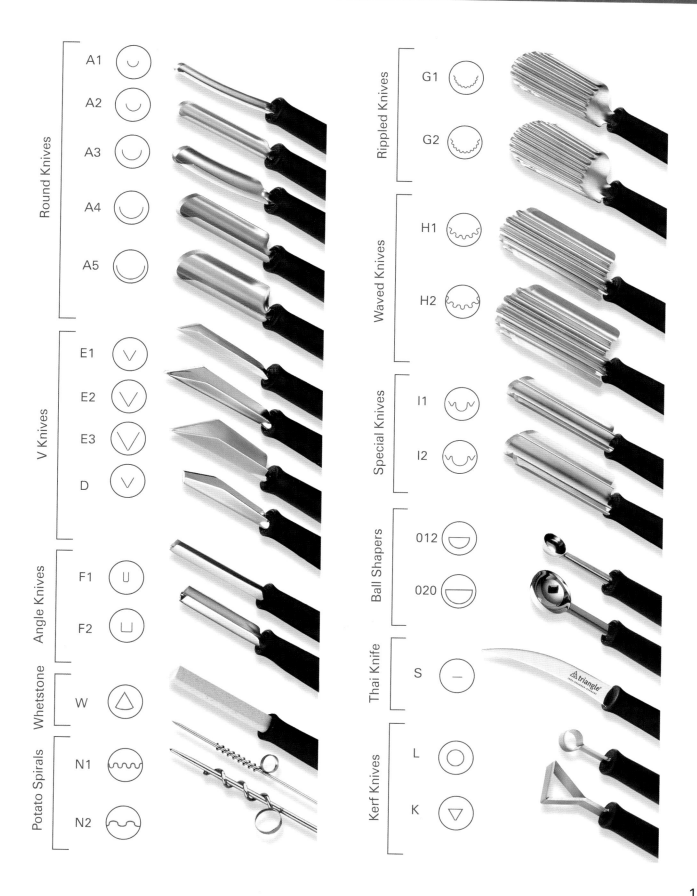

Round Knives
A1
A2
A3
A4
A5

V Knives
E1
E2
E3
D

Angle Knives
F1
F2

Whetstone
W

Potato Spirals
N1
N2

Rippled Knives
G1
G2

Waved Knives
H1
H2

Special Knives
I1
I2

Ball Shapers
012
020

Thai Knife
S

Kerf Knives
L
K

02 The Basics

Flowers and Leaves: Nice Objects to Begin With

To achieve appropriate results when carving vegetables, it is very important to proceed step by step. Even if you are familiar with using general kitchen cutlery, working with carving knives can cause a little trouble at first. What you do with your hands is different and the cutting motion always moves away from your body.

Therefore you should take your time, never rush, begin with the basic elements, and develop your skills gradually. If your basic skills are correct, you will soon be successful. Following this methodology, soon you will reach the point where you can bring your own creativity into your work.

Flower and leaf motifs are especially suited for learning basic skills and how to handle the carving knife. Since you do not need to worry about proportions and shapes when you carve flowers and leaves, like you do when carving animals, you can concentrate exclusively on the technique and how you position the carving tool.

For inexperienced carvers it is easier to practice carving techniques on various types of vegetables and then try the softer fruits. Naturally, all the carving patterns shown here can also be made with fruits.

Daisies and Company

As you take your first steps with fruit and vegetable carving, daisies are simple, radial flowers that are very suitable for getting used to the carving knife. They make fantastic accents as table, plate, or glass decorations. You can combine a variety of carving knives as you wish on these motifs and you can create many kinds of flowers with just a single carving technique. All kinds of firm fruits and vegetables are suitable for creating a wealth of blossoms.

E3

012

Flower Variation 1

01. You need a slice of vegetable or fruit about 1 cm thick. If the slice is not round, shape it with a round cutter (see page 16 for more information on cutters). The more symmetrical the starting shape is, the easier it is to carve even flowers out of it.

02. Cut notches to the middle with the **V knife (E3)** at intervals of about 1 cm. Be sure that the notches meet at the center

and that the width and depth of each notch is even.

03. Using the same knife, cut in just behind the first notches and at a greater angle to the vegetable. Make sure there is not a gap between the carved flower petals and that the cuts meet.

04. Carefully break the edge away and create the middle of the flower by using the **ball shaper (012)**.

01

02
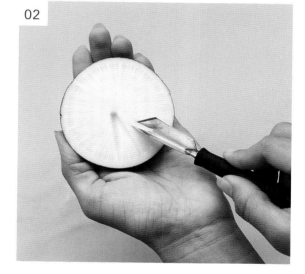

03

04

E2   I1

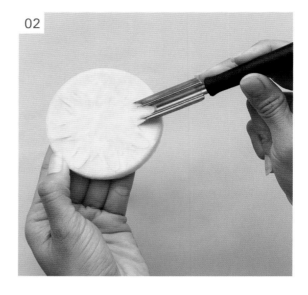

Flower Variation 2

01. For this flower variation, you will also need a round slice (~1 cm thick) of the fruit or vegetable of your choice.

02. Cut inward through the vegetable slice with the **special knife (I1)**. Again, make sure that there are no gaps be-

tween the individual cuts.

03. Carefully break the edge away from the flower.

04. Cut notches between the petals with a **V knife (E1 or E2)**.

A3   012

05

05. Pin a smaller flower with a different color to the middle of the flower with a toothpick.

Flower Variation 3

01. Start with a round slice of a firm vegetable or fruit about 1 cm thick.

02. Make a ring in the middle of the flower by cutting 3 mm deep into the slice with the **round knife (A3)** and then turning the knife.

01

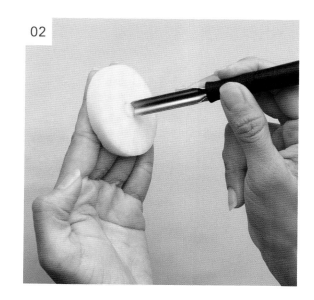

02

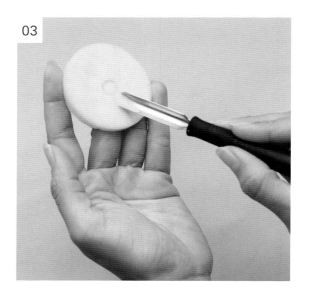

03

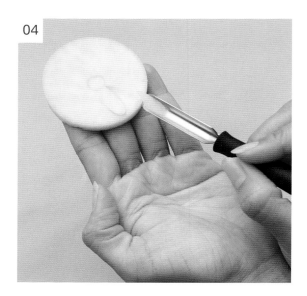

04

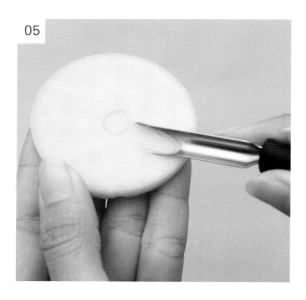

05

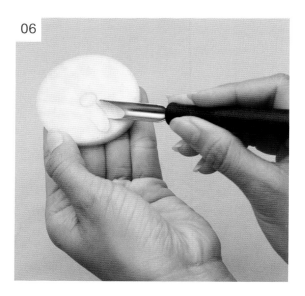

06

03. Turn the **round knife (A3)** against your chosen cutting direction to create this nice marguerite daisy. Make a notch to the middle and turn the knife slightly toward the cutting direction. Do not cut all the way to the middle, so that this piece does not break off.

04. Cut again just beneath the first notch at a larger angle. Cut deeply enough so that you cut through to the bottom.

05. From the second petal on, cut the notches deep enough so they come loose.

06. Make your second cuts according to the shape of the petal and deep enough to cut through the material. Cut each petal around the center in this way.

07. After cutting out the last petal, cut off the first notch you made.

08./09. Break the edge away and insert a flower center.

10. Examples of several flowers carved with this technique and various round knives.

TIP

Be creative and combine various flowers of different sizes and colors to make an attractive bouquet.

Marigolds,

Edelweiss, and Similar Flowers

This section is based on the carving techniques just described. There you learned the basics of fruit and vegetable carving by making radial flowers. With the same technique, you can make more complex flowers that will excite your family and guests. Here, again, you can combine various carving knives as you choose.

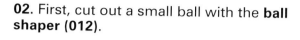

A4   E2   S   012

The following examples will show you how you can also create more complex flowers by yourself. All kinds of firm vegetables and fruits are suitable. These flowers look especially nice when you combine vegetables and fruits in various colors.

Flower Variation 1

01. Use a firm vegetable or fruit of your choice sliced to about 1.5 cm thick. The slice must be somewhat thicker than the daisies because you will be carving two rows of petals for this flower.

02. First, cut out a small ball with the **ball shaper (012)**.

03. Use the **Thai knife** to cut the outer rim away at an angle. The piece should be evenly rounded.

04. With the **V knife (E 2)**, cut small notches at intervals of 5-6 mm.

01

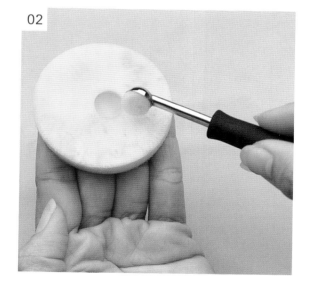

02

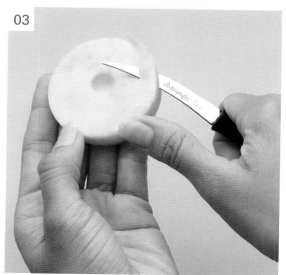

03

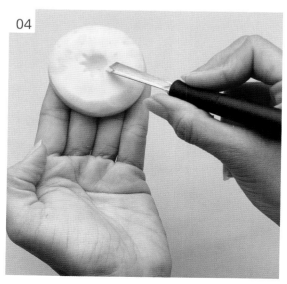

04

05

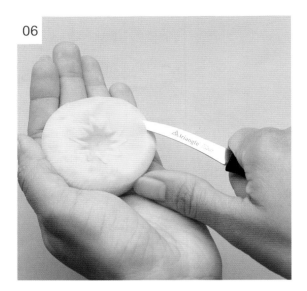

06

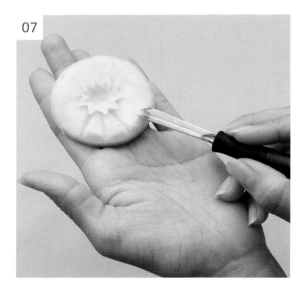

07

08

05. With the same knife, make another series of cuts just behind your initial notches. Cut at a larger angle to the vegetable and cut in only far enough for the individual cuts to meet but not cut through.

06. Make a ring-like cut around the short petals with the **Thai knife** to remove the excess material.

07. On the new layer you have just made with the **Thai knife**, cut notches between the short petals with the V knife. The notches should run from the edge of your material to the middle.

08. Using the **round knife (A4)** at a downward angle, cut all the way through every other notch.

09. Break off the material from under the flower.

10. Cut a small ball out of a fruit or vegetable with a different color using the **ball shaper (012)**. Attach the ball to the middle of the flower with a toothpick or vegetable adhesive.

A1   E2   S

Flower Variation 2

01. Start with a slice of any firm, white vegetable, about 1.5 cm thick.

02. Form a ring in the middle of the flower by sticking a **round knife (A1)** vertically into the vegetable and then turning the knife.

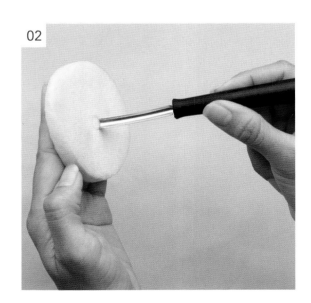

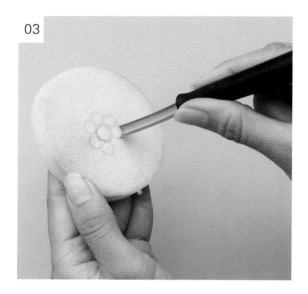

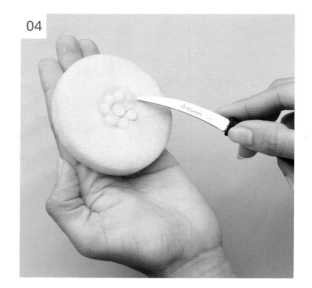

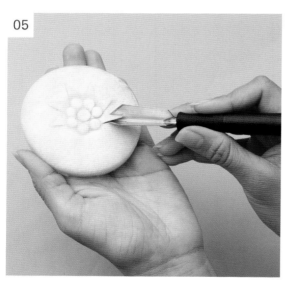

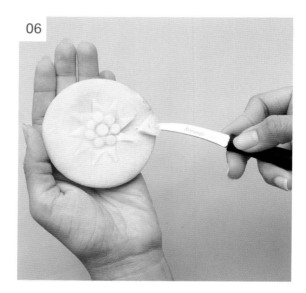

03. Make similar rings around the center ring.

04. Use a **Thai knife** to cut the pulp out from around the rings.

05. Push the **V knife (E2)** about 3 mm into the material at an angle. Repeat this process around the piece. Make the cuts deep enough so that they reach the rings.

06. Cut out the pulp between the cuts with the **Thai knife**.

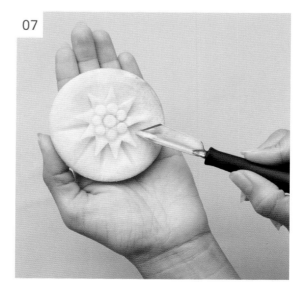

07. With the **V knife (E2)**, cut notches inward from the outer rim and between the petals

08. Cut all the way through the pulp below the notches.

09./**10**. Break the edge away.

11. Examples of various flowers produced with this carving technique, using various carving knives.

TIP

To present your flowers, drive nails into a root or other piece of wood and cut off the nail heads. This display makes a perfect centerpiece or an accent for a buffet table.

08

09

10

11

Leaves

Zucchini, cucumbers, yellow beets, and carrots are ideal for making leaves. Multi-colored pumpkin and melon rinds also work well. If you would rather use fruits to make leaves, apples look especially nice.

E2   S

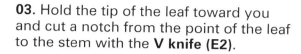

Leaf Variation 1

We will cut the simplest and fastest variation first.

01. Cut pieces off a zucchini large enough to hold the pattern cutter you have chosen.

02. Use the cutter to create the basic shape of the leaf.

03. Hold the tip of the leaf toward you and cut a notch from the point of the leaf to the stem with the **V knife (E2)**.

04. Cut smaller notches from the outside of the leaf to the main notch you just carved. These notches should run forward on the leaf at an angle. Repeat this step on both sides of the main rib.

01

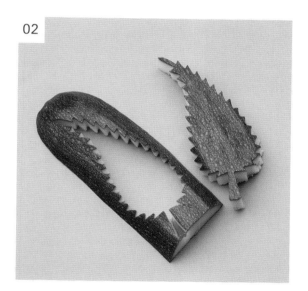

02

03

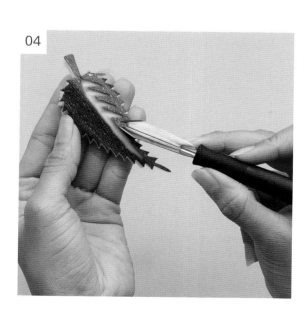

04

E2
S

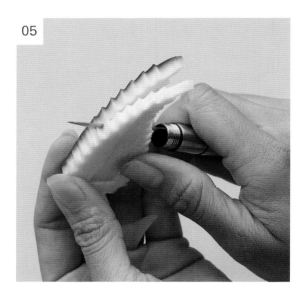

05

05. Finally, use the **Thai knife** to cut off the excess pulp from the bottom of the leaf. This gives the leaf a nice, thin shape.

TIP

Carved leaves add charm to carved flowers. But single leaves work well as plate decorations.

Leaf Variation 2

To create this type of leaf, you need two more techniques. As an alternative to the **V knife (E2)**, you can also make the notches with the **kerf (K)** or **Thai knife**, which is demonstrated in the following pictures.

01. First, using the **Thai knife**, make two cuts about 2 mm apart from the stem to the tip.

02. Next, hold the knife at an angle and cut a thin strip out of the leaf that runs parallel to your first cut. This creates the main rib of the leaf.

01

02

S

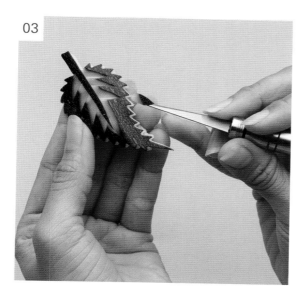

03. You can cut the leaf veins out with either the **V knife (E2)** or the **Thai knife**. Then use the **Thai knife** to cut away the excess pulp on the bottom of the leaf so that the leaf is nice and flat.

Leaf Variation 3

01. With the **Thai knife**, cut out small ovals from the leaf, moving outward from the central rib. If the white pulp is still visible, hold the knife to the leaf at an angle. If you cut the ovals all the way through, you can try holding the knife perpendicular to the leaf when you cut.

02. Repeat this step on the other side of the leaf. Make sure that the ovals run forward at an angle and become somewhat smaller toward the front. Then use the **Thai knife** to cut off the excess pulp on the bottom.

35

Dahlias

To carve dahlias and similar flowers, you need carving knives of different sizes.
Always cut rows of petals starting with the smallest inside row and move to the
outside. Since the size of the vegetable increases with every row, you should use in-
crementally larger carving knives as you work outward. The petals of the dahlias are
either right under each other or alternating. Dahlia flowers look especially nice when
they are made of whole melons or pumpkins. Here various knife shapes are used.

E1, E2

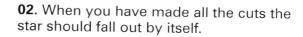

Various types of fruits and vegetables are suitable for these striking flowers, for example, radishes, red and yellow beets, kohlrabi, zucchini, melons, mangoes, apples, and round black radishes.

Flower Variation 1
Radishes

01. Cut a small star into the radish with a small **V knife (E1)**. You will need about six cuts with a small radish and eight with a larger one. Always work from the outside to the inside, which helps make the lengths of your cuts equal.

02. When you have made all the cuts the star should fall out by itself.

03. Leaving a thin, red border, cut a little deeper under the points of the star. Do not leave any gaps between the cuts. Now the first row of petals is finished.

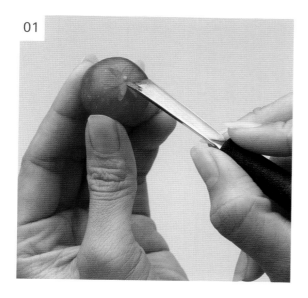

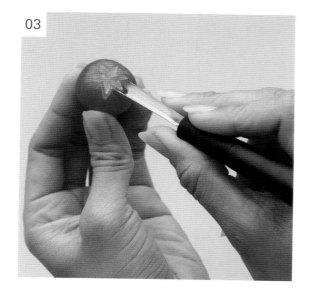

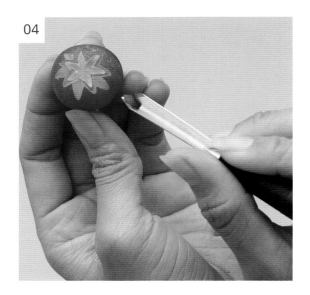

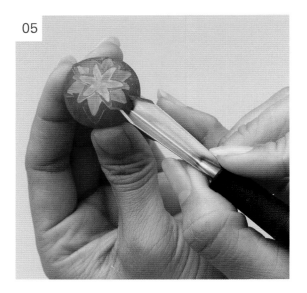

04. With the same **V knife (E1)**, cut between the petals again. Begin somewhat farther down and move the knife upward at an angle to the previous cuts. Again, the piece should fall out by itself.

05. Leave another thin red border and make the secondary cuts with a larger **V knife (E2)**. This completes the second row of petals. Depending on the size of the radish you can cut several rows of petals.

A1-A5   012

Flower Variation 2
Black Radish

01. For this flower, use all the **round knives (A1-A5)** and the **ball shaper (012)**.

02. Cut a hemisphere out of the middle of the radish with the **ball shaper (012)**.

03. Using the smallest of the **round knives (A1)**, cut downward at an angle around the circle at regular intervals.

01

02
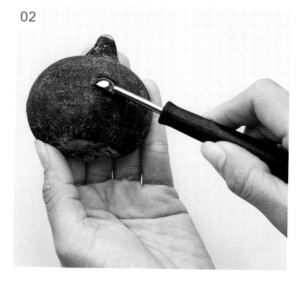

03

makes the petals stronger than the outside ones and prevents them from breaking off easily. Make sure that the individual cuts match up and there are no gaps.

05. With the same **round knife**, cut the pulp away directly between each petal. Hold the knife as flat as you can, so as not to cut deeper than 1 mm into the vegetable.

04. Leave a thin border and cut downward at an angle right behind your initial cuts. Hold the **round knife** at a steeper angle than the previous cuts, which

06

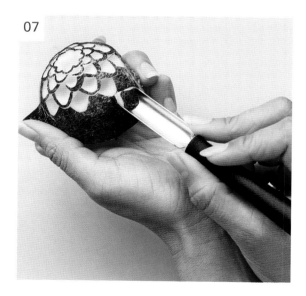

07

08

06. Again, leave a thin, dark border and cut in about 1 mm deep just behind the previous one with the **round knife (A2)**. Make sure there are no gaps between the individual cuts.

07. Continue to make rows of petals with this technique. When making your second way around a row, be sure to use the same **round knife** that you used for the initial cuts. However, use the next largest **round knife** when moving to the next row of petals.

08. Here we show you an assortment of various flowers made with this technique.

TIP

With two-tone vegetables, always leave a thin border of rind to create a nice color effect. With monochromatic vegetables, such as kohlrabi, cut the outer petals as thin as possible. The deeper you carve the flowers, the more contrast and effect you create. Of course it also becomes more difficult to carve the individual cuts simply and evenly.

Water Lilies and Dandelions
Flower Petals Carved with One Knife

For this type of flower, one knife is sufficient for all the petals in the blossom, which are cut out from the inside. When you cut with the Thai knife, you must be very careful not to cut away petals by mistake. Thus it is important to make sure that the vegetables and fruits you use are firm and not too fibrous.

Flower Variation 1
Water Lily in Yellow Beet

01. Here you need a large **round knife (A5)** for the center point, the **V knife**, and the **Thai knife**.

02. With the round carving knife, cut into the pulp about 1 cm deep and turn the knife to make a ring.

03. Trim a ring around the center point with the **Thai knife** that is 1 cm deep and 1 cm wide.

04. Round the edges of the center point with the **Thai knife**.

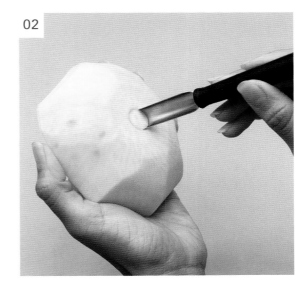

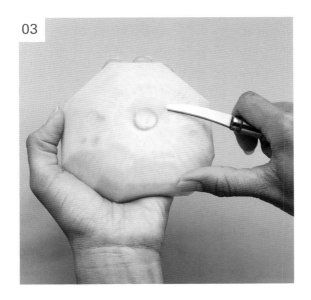

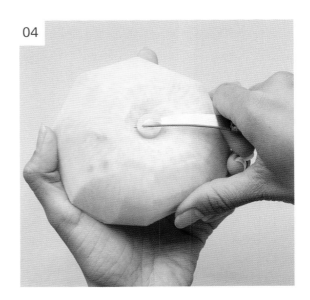

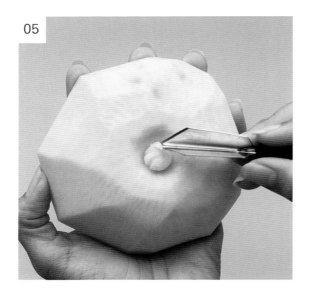

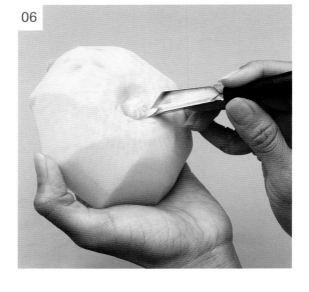

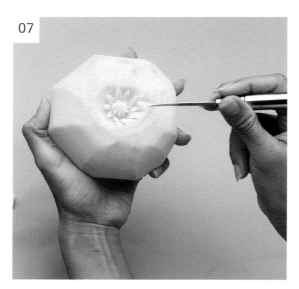

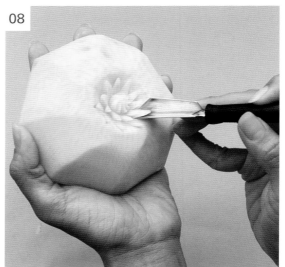

05. Cut notches into and around the center point with the **V knife (E2)**.

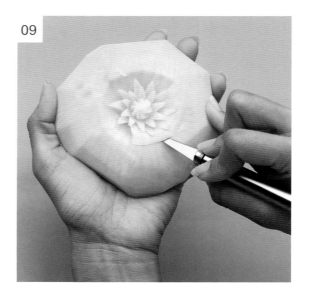

06. Use the same knife to cut downward and at an angle into the space around the center point. Make sure there are no gaps between individual cuts.

07. With the **Thai knife**, carefully cut another 1 cm ring around the layer of petals you just carved. Remove the strip of pulp from the piece.

08. In the ring you just created, carve all around the beet as in step **06**.

Level of Difficulty ★ ★ ☆

Tools used for Flower Variation 2, plus toothpick or vegetable pin.

E2   S   012

09. Carefully cut out another ring with the **Thai knife**.

10. Repeat these steps row after row.

11. Carefully break away the edge of the blossom. If the edge is resistant in any spots, cut it with the **Thai knife**.

Flower Variation 2

01. For this flower, use a **ball shaper (012)** for the center point, the **V knife (E2)**, and the **Thai knife**.

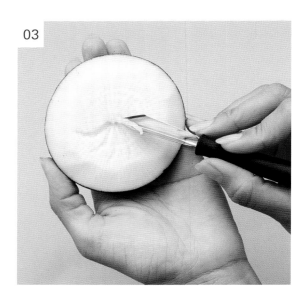

02. Round off the outer rim with the **Thai knife**.

03. Cut curved notches to the center with the **V knife (E2)**.

04. Follow these notches with a row of notches that comes in beneath the first set at a greater angle to the vegetable. Keep the same curved pattern and make sure there are no gaps between the cuts. Otherwise the excess material will not fall out in the next step.

05. Cut a ring about 5 mm deep around the outer edge of the vegetable with the **Thai knife**.

06. Cut another set of curved notches with the **V knife**, this time in the opposite direction.

07. Cut in behind the notches again with a turning motion, making sure not to leave any gaps. Remove the pulp underneath with the **Thai knife** and repeat this process for a few more rows.

08. Break the edge away.

09. Make the center of the flower with a toothpick or vegetable pin.

10. Various flowers made with this carving technique

TIP

Flowers carved with the small V knife are very attractive. But be careful, the delicate petals break off very easily.

Asters

To make asters, the cutting moves from the outside in. For flowers with more than one row of petals, begin with the outermost row.

The two examples shown here feature two different flowers: a variation with just one row of petals and one with several rows. For these flowers, do not use fruits and vegetables that are too soft. The ends of radishes, cucumbers, and green papayas are very suitable.

D   S

After cutting, be sure to put your radish in cold water, which helps make the individual petals firm. The shape of **V knife (D)** is particularly suited for curving cuts (see Variation 1).

Flower Variation 1
Radish: Flower with One Row of Petals

01. Make sure that the radish is not too small and has a nice round shape. Remove roots and leaves with the **Thai knife**.

02./03. With the **V knife (D)**, cut curving lines from one pole of the radish to the other. Make sure the cuts are very even and leave some of the radish rind visible between the cuts.

01

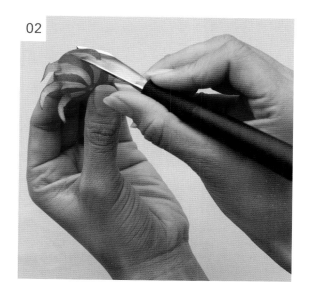

02

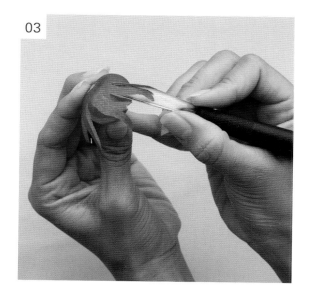

03

E2   S

Keep the individual petals on cucumbers firm by placing the vegetable in cold water after cutting.

Flower Variation 2
Cucumber: Flower with two or more rows of petals

01. Cut a 7-8 cm piece off the end of a cucumber.

02. Make grooves with a **V knife (E2)** lengthwise in the cucumber. Make sure that all the grooves are equally deep. The grooves must meet at the lower end of the cucumber. If there is a gap between the grooves, you will have trouble removing the pulp in the next step.

03. Use the **Thai knife** to remove the remaining skin from the cucumber, leaving a clean, even surface.

01

02

03

04. The outer row of petals is finished.

05. Cut a 0.5 cm slice off the end of the cucumber with the **Thai knife**.

TIP

The longer the vegetable is the greater impact the individual petals will have. However, with longer pieces the cutting becomes more difficult.

06

06. Repeat step 02 to make a second row of petals, this time cutting into the meat of the cucumber.

07. Remove the excess cucumber from your flower with a twist of your hand.

07

08

08. Using a toothpick, attach a smaller flower with a different color in the center of the cucumber star.

09. With this technique you can make flowers from several types of fruits and vegetables, such as papaya, radish, and cucumber.

09

Easy
Plate Decorations

With our easy ideas for plate decorations you can carve accents for a dinner to effectively reinforce a delicious meal.

Plate Variation 1
Tiny Ears of Corn

01. Cut a piece of yellow beet or carrot about 5 cm long and 2 cm wide into an oval shape with the **Thai knife**.

02. With the **Thai knife**, cut thin slits along four adjacent sides of the piece, to about 0.5 cm from the end. The flesh under the slits will become the corn kernels.

03. Cut lines with the **kerf knife (K)**, first along the length of the ear, and then across at right angles to your first lines.

04. Colorful corn ears with cucumber leaves—a nice, easy plate decoration.

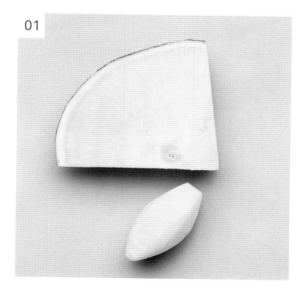

01

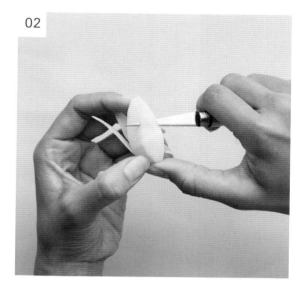

02

03

04

S

01

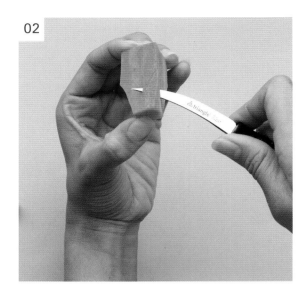

02

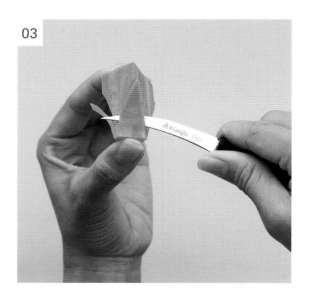

03

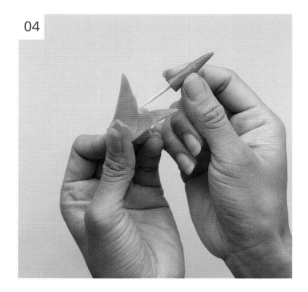

04

Plate Variation 2
Flowers Made of Carrot and Chili

01. You will need a piece of carrot about 6-8 cm long and one small red chili pepper for this decoration. Cut a triangular column out of the carrot.

02. Cut the angles in to create the petals.

03. Cut the petals to 2 mm thick at each corner. Loosen the excess carrot away from the flower with the **Thai knife**.

04. Place a small piece of red chili pepper into the flower with a toothpick.

E1   012

Plate Variation 3
Flowers on a Leaf

01. Here you will need a slice of white vegetable about 1 cm thick, a smaller slice of carrot, and a small ball of yellow beet cut with the **ball shaper (012)**. Press flowers out with pattern cutters that fit your vegetable slices.

02. Cut grooves along the flower petals with the small **V knife (E1)**.

03. Stack the individual parts of the flower on top of one another and decorate the piece with a carved leaf of your choice (see page 32).

04. The completed decoration with a leaf.

K

Plate Variation 4
Cucumber Ornament with Radish Flower

01. You need a piece of cucumber, cut in half lengthwise.

02. With the **kerf knife (K)**, make grooves lengthwise about 1 cm apart.

03. With a **vegetable knife** cut seven, 1mm thick slices. Remove this piece from the rest of the cucumber.

01

02

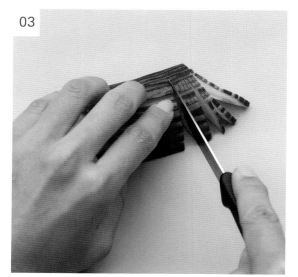

03

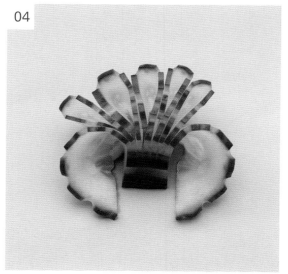

04

05

04. Bend the two outer leaves to face forward and fluff the rest of the leaves in the back.

05. A few more suggestions for similar decorations made of cucumber.

06. Flower and leaf—a colorful plate decoration. You will find directions for making the radish flower on page 37.

06

Cocktail Decorations

With a few carving skills and some creativity, you can astound your guests with delightful cocktail decorations. You only need a few small pattern cutters and some simple carving techniques to let your creativity loose.

Here we show you several ideas for decorations that employ techniques found in this book. Fruit decorations are ideal for most drinks, but a Bloody Mary, for example, should have a celery stalk and vegetable. It is best to garnish your drinks with tasteful types of fruits and vegetables.

03 Little Works of Art
Objects for Any Season

While you should work very systematically and linearly when you carve, some flowers, animals, and ornaments should be developed with a certain amount of spatial thinking. It is important to adhere to proportions and include fine details when carving figures. To be sure, only a few people have the talent to carve a finished bird in a piece of radish free hand.

Thus we have assembled patterns for you that should help make your work easier. Cut the patterns out of the appendix and place them on your fruits and vegetables to create an outline for your carving work. The patterns will provide you with the basic shape, proportions, and details you will need to carve the figure. Drawings from children's books also make very good patterns for small works of art. They are much better than photos because the art is reduced to the essential lines and are often presented strongly overdrawn.

Get inspired by the following edible decorations that we have assembled according to seasons and events!

Spring Greetings

For this splendid spring bouquet you can select various colorful flowers from the previous chapter (page 18). The vase for this arrangement is a star made out of a cantaloupe, which you will find on the next page. A sun of yellow vegetables and a few butterflies finish the ensemble. Naturally, you can also use these lovely elements individually for decorative purposes. Use a sponge or a piece of firm vegetable (kohlrabi works best) to arrange your carved objects. Cut your medium so it fits perfectly into the melon vessel.

A1

D

S

01

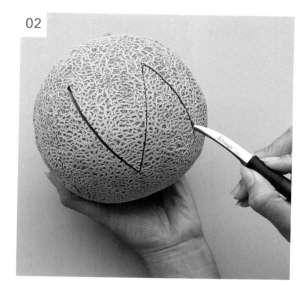

02

03

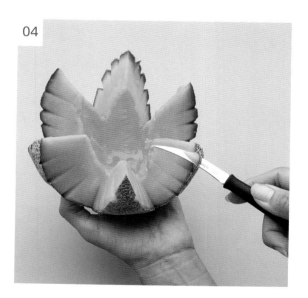

04

A Vase Made of Cantaloupe

01. Make sure that your melon is firm and evenly shaped. You can carve two melon stars out of one melon.

02. With the **Thai knife**, cut a large zig-zag pattern into the melon. You should have about six points on each half of the melon.

03. With the **melon scoop** (or a soup spoon), remove the pulp from the melon.

04. Next, use the **Thai knife** to cut fine notches on all sides of the points. They should not be too deep.

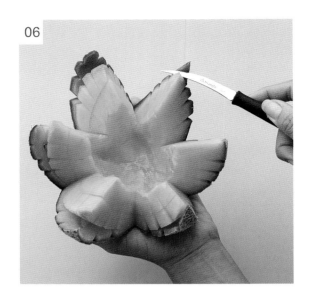

05. Make two cuts into each point with the **Thai knife**.

06. With the same knife, cut the meat along the bowl from the top all the way to the lower edge of the points. Make sure the cuts are the same on all the points. The rind on the rim of the bowl should not be more than 2-3 mm thick. If it is too thick, the points will be very stiff and will not bend easily.

07./08. Pull the outer part of each point downward. It should look like an opened flower.

The Butterfly

01. Start with a slice of firm vegetable about 0.5 cm thick. We are using a yellow beet. Use a large butterfly cutter to create the basic form of the decoration.

02. With the **Thai knife**, cut a small wedge-shaped piece from either side, between the body and wings.

03. Cut two grooves across the butterfly's body with the **Thai knife**. Then cut structural lines into both wings with the **round knife (A1)**.

04. Turn the butterfly to the side and use the **Thai knife** to thin the wings by cutting some pulp away from the underside.

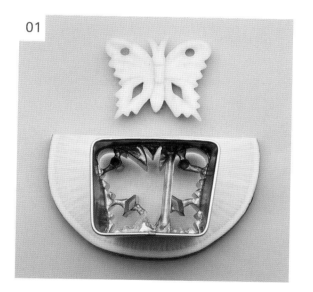

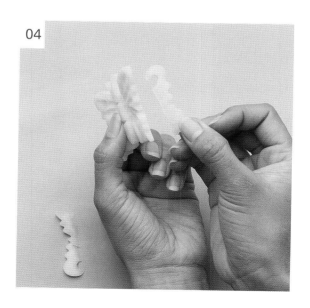

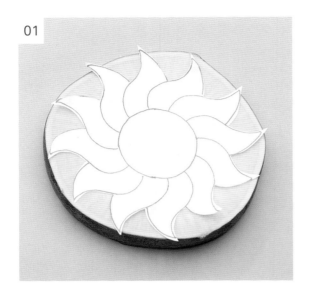

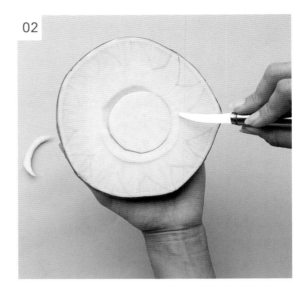

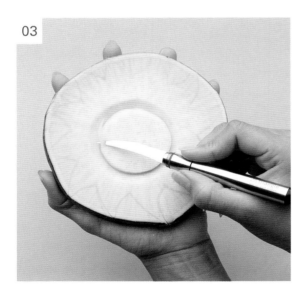

The Sun

01. Use a slice of yellow beet about 1 cm thick. Copy the pattern from page 123, scale it to fit on the slice, and cut it out. Moisten the pattern a bit and place it on the vegetable slice.

02. With the **Thai knife**, cut the outline of the sun into the vegetable. Then cut a ring 0.5 cm deep for the center of the sun. Make a groove around the ring, holding the knife at about a 45-degree angle.

03. Round off the top edge of the center.

04. Cut completely through the outline of the sun and remove the excess.

05

06

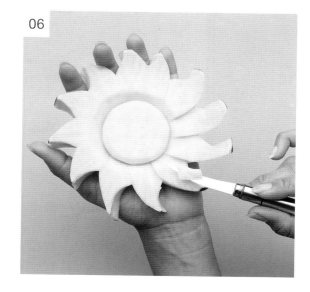

05. Lengthen the lines leading into the center with cuts about 0.5 cm deep. Cut into the vegetable vertically.

06. Cut from the left side diagonally to the cutout so that the wedge-shaped piece falls out.

07. Use the **V knife (D)** to cut grooves along the rays to the center. This will make the sun look more decorative.

Now you can begin to combine flowers, leaves, sun, and butterfly imaginatively into a beautiful and colorful bouquet.

07

TIP

The toothpicks and skewers that you use to display your decoration should not be visible to the observer. As an alternative to using toothpicks, gather a variety of very fine twigs and attach the vegetable flowers to them with adhesive. This gives the arrangement a nice natural air.

Gentleman
in Tailcoat

This figure is easy to make and is a real attention-getter, especially for children's birthday parties. When shopping, make sure to purchase eggplants that are as thin and straight as possible.

01
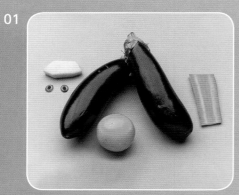

02

03

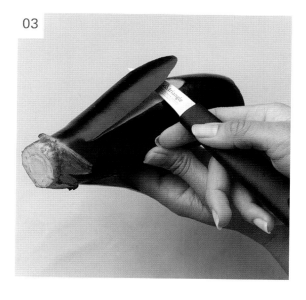

04

05

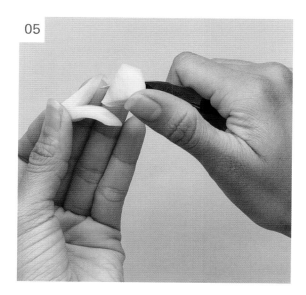

01. Use thin eggplants, a piece of yellow beet, a piece of carrot, a small mandarin orange, and two small radish discs for eyes. For the pupils, stick two small discs of eggplant onto the radish discs.

02. Cut off both ends of the eggplant with a **vegetable knife** or the **Thai knife**. With the same knife, cut a flat piece off one side of the eggplant. This will be the front of the bird.

03. To create the wings, turn the eggplant 90 degrees and make a flat, upward cut to the top of the eggplant. Stop about 3-4 cm from the top of the vegetable so you do not cut the piece all the way off. This space will also prevent the wing from breaking off. Turn the eggplant to the other side and repeat this step to make the second wing.

04. Using a toothpick, stick a mandarin orange onto the top of the eggplant to make the head.

05. Cut the bird's beak out of a piece of yellow beet.

TIP

With this technique you can make various animals and characters out of fruits and vegetables. Look through some children's books for inspiration.

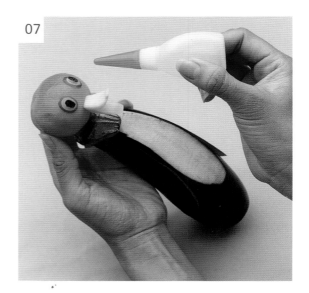

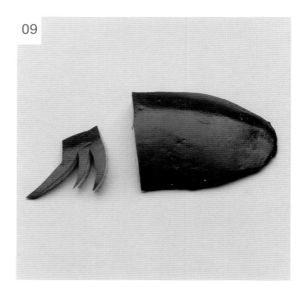

06./07. Attach the beak to the head with a toothpick. Apply the two eyes with vegetable adhesive.

08./09. Make the top hat out of the second eggplant. With the **vegetable knife**, cut a slice about 1 cm thick from the widest part of the eggplant and a section about 5 cm long from the narrowest part. Attach the two pieces to the bird's head with a toothpick. Now you only need two tufts of hair. Cut these out of a thin piece of eggplant.

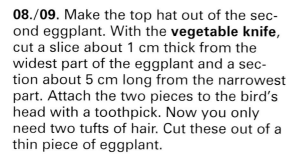

10. Adhere the hair on the left and right sides, between the head and top hat, with vegetable adhesive.

11. Now our feathered gentleman needs feet. Cut these out of two thin pieces of eggplant with the **Thai knife** and attach them to the bird with toothpicks. Make the tie and bowtie out of pieces of carrot and yellow beet that are about 5 mm thick. Cut out the basic shape of these items with the **Thai knife** and round off the outer edges a bit.

12. With the small **V knife (E1),** cut a few notches into the bowtie.

13. Attach the bird's final articles of clothing with a toothpick.

14. Voila—the fished work of art!

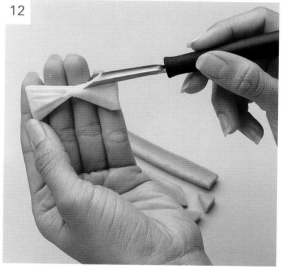

The
Coral Reef

This colorful coral reef with bright tropical fish looks impressive and is relatively easy to make with a little practice. It is the ideal summer decoration and will put your guests in the mood for a vacation! Cucumber asters (you will find the directions on page 50) complete the dreamy underwater world.

A1 A2   D   S

01. For the actual coral reef you will need ginger, sunchoke (Jerusalem artichoke), and lotus root. Use toothpicks and wooden skewers to combine the various elements.

02. Using the skewers, stick several larger pieces of ginger and sunchoke together to create a basic structure for the reef. This provides the needed stability.

03. Add cut pieces of lotus root to create a remarkably realistic coral reef.

04. Add a few asters made of cucumber (see page 50) to represent sea anemones.

TIP

Compared to other animals, fish are quite easy to carve, especially because there are so many different kinds. Nothing should stand in the way of your creativity. But always make sure that the basic shape of the fish has lively curves so it does not look stiff. Fish with big fins generally look better.

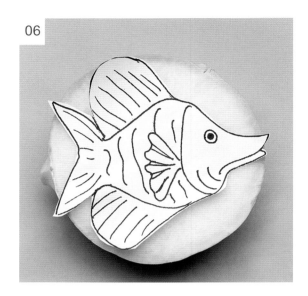

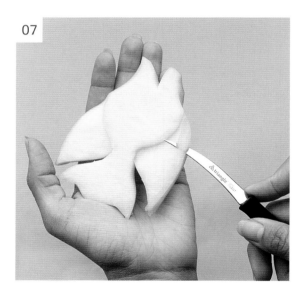

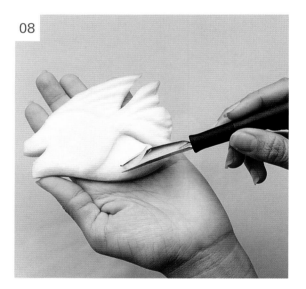

05. For the fish, use a slice of vegetable that is 1.5 cm thick. Kohlrabi, yellow beet, and pumpkin all work well. Copy the pattern from page 122 if you would like, or try to make your own fish design.

06. Put the pattern, slightly dampened, on the vegetable and cut along the outer lines of the fish with the **Thai knife**.

07. Divide the fish's body and the fins, making the fins thinner than the body. Round off the fins a bit from both sides with the **Thai knife**.

08. With the **V knife**, cut notches in all the fins. Make sure that the notches always run toward the fish's body.

09. Cut the gill cover with the **Thai knife**. Make a round cut from top to bottom and cut behind it, holding the knife at a sharp angle to remove a wedge-shaped piece of pulp.

10. Shape the eye by inserting and turning the **round knife (A1)**.

11. Use the **Thai knife** to cut out pulp from around the eye (1-2 mm deep).

12. Place a black peppercorn as the pupil. Glue it in with vegetable adhesive if necessary.

13. With the **Thai knife**, cut very thin strips to make the upper and lower lips.

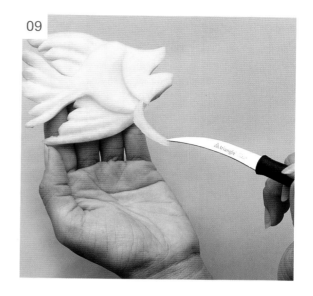

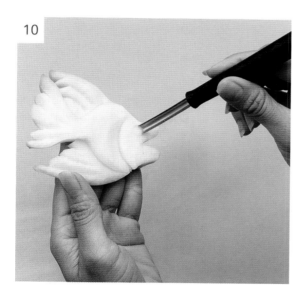

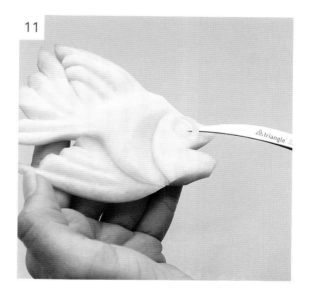

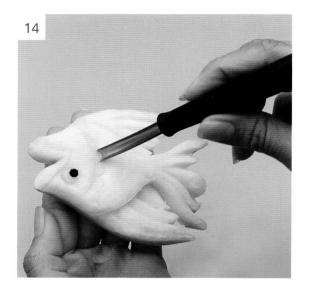

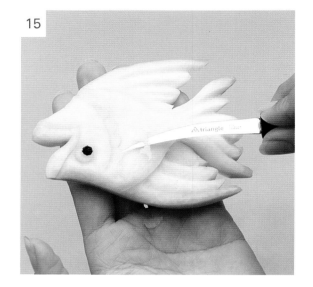

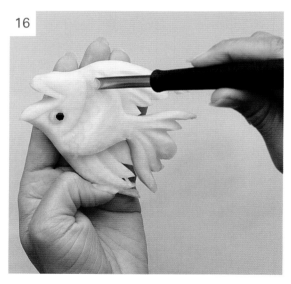

14. Carve the fish's scales by sticking the second-smallest **round knife (A2)** 3 mm into the vegetable. Start behind the gill cover and make sure that the scales form rows without gaps.

15. With the **Thai knife**, cut a thin strip of pulp from behind each scale. Hold the tip of the knife at a small angle to the vegetable.

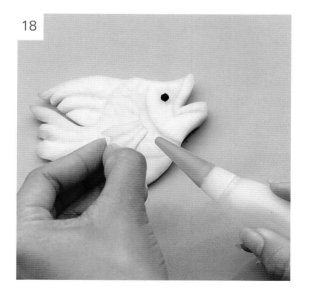

16. Repeat the last two steps until the fish's body is completely covered with scales. Make sure that the rows of scales alternate with each other.

17. Cut a fin out of the remaining pieces of fruit pulp.

18. Stick the fin onto the fish behind the gill cover.

19. You can also decorate the coral reef with red chili pepper flowers to make it more colorful. To do this, cut the chili pepper in half.

20. With the **Thai knife**, cut lengthwise into the middle of the pepper.

21. Cut the seeds out of the pepper.

22. Skewer the end piece of the chili pepper on a toothpick and stick it into the piece with the petals. Place the chili flower in cold water. It will "blossom" in a short period of time. After you have attached the fish to the coral reef with wooden skewers, place the chili flowers in the arrangement.

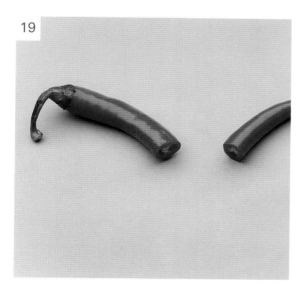

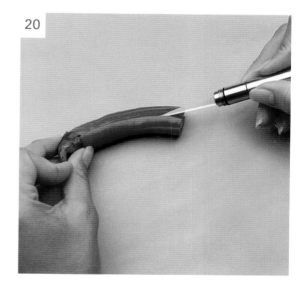

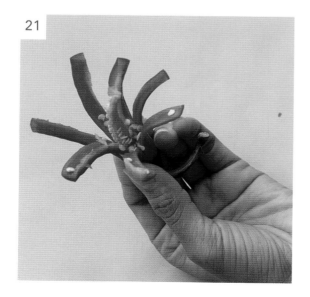

Carving Melons

Melons are the most popular fruits for carving. If the meat is nice and firm they are relatively easy to carve. They are also very decorative thanks to their size and variety of colors. Thus, when you carve a melon you should always make sure to include all the colors of the fruit in the carving. For example, dark green watermelon rind offers a fine contrast to the red of its pulp. You should use this contrast in your carved objects to make them as rich as possible.

Since the rind is the hardest part, you must be very careful with the carving knives. Avoid using too much pressure so you do not slip through the softer pulp into the seed core.

If the melon is already very ripe it is best to carve it with a **Thai knife**. Using a larger carving knife causes more pressure when cutting and presses the pulp into a shapeless mass.

You should also take notice of the seeds. With watermelons it is best to use those with few or no seeds. With other melons it is important not to cut in too deeply when carving, which makes the melon look very unsightly.

If you keep to these criteria you will have a melon that is ideal for a variety of carving techniques—a fruit that you can use to create a splendid decoration

Watermelon
Fruit Bowl

What would a hot summer day be without fresh fruit!
This bowl, however, is not made of porcelain, but rather carved out of a juicy
melon. You can fill it with a fruit salad or even strawberries dipped in chocolate.

A5   E1-E3   G1-G2   H1-H2   S   K

01

02
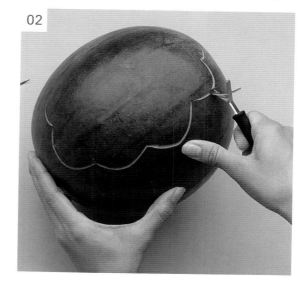

03

04
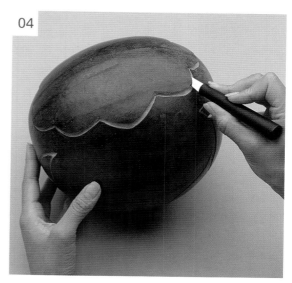

01. Choose a melon with a dark green rind to create rich contrast in your carving.

02. With the **kerf knife (K)**, sketch the line on the melon's rind where you will cut the top off.

03. Using the same knife, sketch in a leaf pattern on the front of the melon, near the bottom.

04. With the **Thai knife**, cut the top off along the marked line.

05. Leaving a slight border at the top of the melon, use the **Thai knife** to remove the rind in the area between the top border and the leaves at the bottom.

05
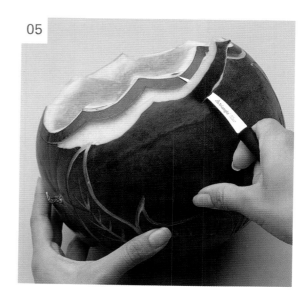

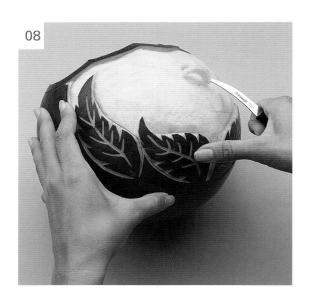

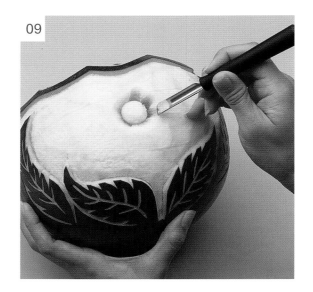

06. Cut the details of the leaves.

07. Using the largest **round knife (A5)**, cut a circle about 1 cm wide and 1.5 cm deep in the middle of the peeled surface.

08. With the **Thai knife**, cut a ring about 1 cm wide and 1.5 cm deep around the circle.

09./10. Use the various round, ridged, and rippled knives to carve a flower as you did in the section on dahlias (page 36).

11. With the medium **V knife (E2)**, carve grooves around the edge of the peeled area beneath the outermost petals.

12. Carve the same pattern you used for the side of the bowl into the top. But instead of the **round knife**, use the various **V knives (E1-E3)** to create a flower with pointed petals. To make use of all the melon's colors, always leave a thin border about 2 mm wide on the petals. With the **kerf knife (K)**, carve grooves along the outer edge of the top.

13. Hollow out 2 cm of the melon flesh using a **melon spoon**.

14. Fill the bowl with nicely arranged fruits and attach the top to the bowl with a toothpick.

Honeydew
Flower

This beautifully carved melon is made using Asian carving techniques and will enrich any table or buffet with its charm. A few small leaves for decorative purposes help create even more atmosphere. Get inspired with a trip to the florist.

A1-A3   S

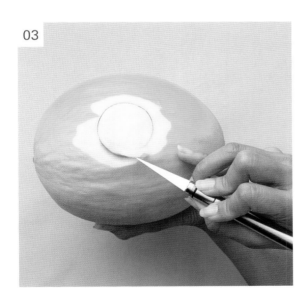

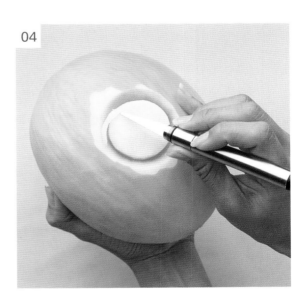

01. Select a very firm, shapely honey-dew melon.

02. Peel a small area in the middle of the melon and cut a circle about 1.5 cm deep with the **circular cutter**. This will mark the center of the flower and define the area for the inner bud and outer petals. If the melon offers resistance, use a turning motion to make your cut.

03. With the **Thai knife**, cut a ring about 1 cm wide around the center bud. Hold the knife at a 45-degree angle to the fruit.

04. Now round the inside edges of the bud. Here too, cut at a 45-degree angle all the way around the edge.

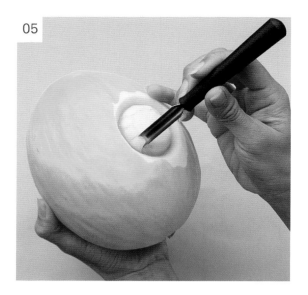

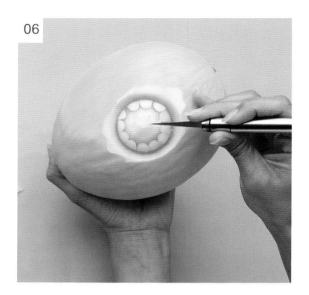

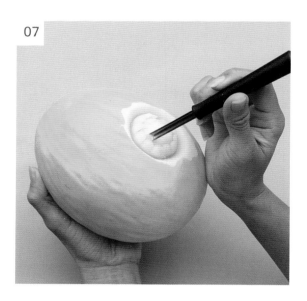

05. Take the smallest of the four **round knives (A1)** and make impressions around the inside edge of the center bud. Hold the knife at a right angle to the melon and position the knife so the rounded edge faces the middle of the bud. Make sure the individual petals meet and there are no gaps between the cuts.

06. With the **Thai knife**, cut out a ring about 1 cm deep from the center of the bud—hold the knife at an angle.

07. Repeat step 05 with the second smallest **round knife (A2)** to make another row of petals.

08. Carve another ring out as in step 06 and repeat step 05 with a third row of petals.

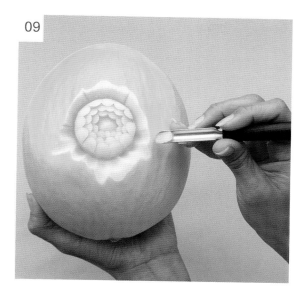

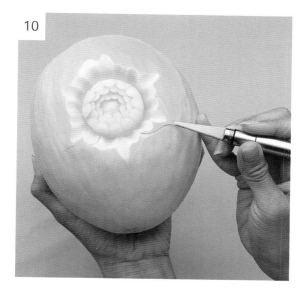

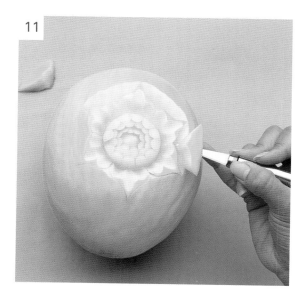

09. After finishing the center bud, start cutting the outer flower petals. Using the **Thai knife**, divide the circumference around the center bud into six equal parts. Take the second largest **round knife (A3)** and cut a long notch into the middle of each part, plus a smaller notch to the right and left. These cuts should always point toward the bud in the middle.

10. Now take the **Thai knife** and cut in a heart-shape about 1 cm deep around these three cuts. Bring the point of the heart shape to end just above the longer notch in the center.

11. Angle the **Thai knife** toward the center of the flower and cut about 1 cm deep to remove the melon between the points of each petal.

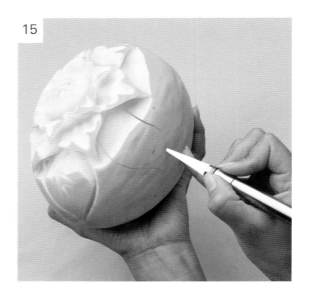

12.-14. Now cut a second row of petals, repeating steps 09 to **11**. Place the second row of petals between the petals in the first row so the pattern alternates.

15. Add a border of leaves to frame the flower. Use the **Thai knife** to cut out a curved leaf shape about 1 cm deep between the petals in your last row. Start the leaf by cutting underneath the petals in the last row.

16. Remove a 5 cm wide edge from both sides of each leaf so that it stands free.

17. To place veins in the petal, use the **Thai knife** and cut a fine wedge-shaped strip in the middle, down the length of the leaf.

18. Then make several small cuts to the left and right of it, running diagonally forward.

19. Depending on the size of your melon, cut as many leaves as possible to form a good setting for the flower.

TIP

You can use all kinds of melons for this carved design. This technique also looks very nice on papaya.

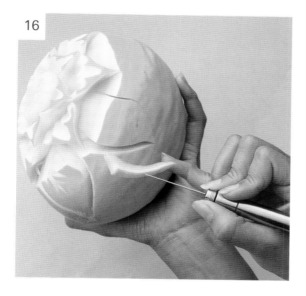

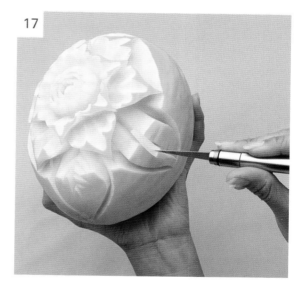

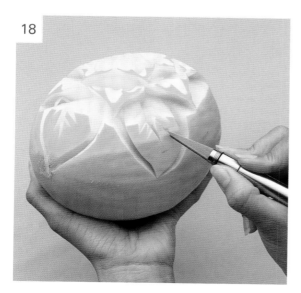

Autumn is Pumpkin Season

Pumpkins and squashes are among the most popular vegetables for carving. Available in a variety of shapes and colors, you can create extremely attractive decorations with these gourds. In addition, pumpkins stay fresh for a long time and will attractively maintain your carvings for several weeks.

When choosing a carving pumpkin you should always select one that is good and firm. It should not give in when pressed and it should not show any damage—those areas will soon go bad. The consistency and hardness of the flesh can vary depending on the vegetable. For example, the hard flesh of a Hokkaido is somewhat harder to work than a Muscat pumpkin. Though most types are only available seasonally, you can now buy the Muscat type almost all year long.

Carved pumpkins and squashes are best wrapped in plastic wrap. Never put them completely in water for any length of time because they will become mushy.

"Pumpkin Time" (opposite)

Witch's Magic

For this Halloween pumpkin, use a pattern to carve the witch motif into the rind. You will find an idea for one on page 125, but you can also give your own imagination free rein. The carved pumpkin lasts up to two weeks and guarantees a fortnight of horror.

01

02

D

S

03

04

05

06

01. Copy the pattern to fit the size of the chosen pumpkin. Halloween pumpkins are best suited, but you could also use a smooth Muscat or Hokkaido pumpkin.

02. Moisten the pattern a bit and press it lightly onto the pumpkin so that it sticks. Cut the outline of the pattern about 2-3 mm deep into the gourd with the **Thai knife**.

03. Use a fine needle to make perforated guidelines along the interior lines of the pattern.

04. Cut the rind in a circular ring around the witch using the **Thai knife**.

05. Make sure that you always cut to the same depth, including the elements (broom, bat) that are outside the cutout border, where the rind has not yet been removed.

06. Use the small **V knife (D)** to make grooves along the lines that were perforated with the needle. Move the **V knife** along the markings on the surface to cut at an even depth.

95

Squash Hedgehog

A butternut squash is best suited for this thorny cavalier. You should make sure that the fruit has grown straight and the upper part has almost the same width as the lower part.

E1-E3   S   012/020

01

02

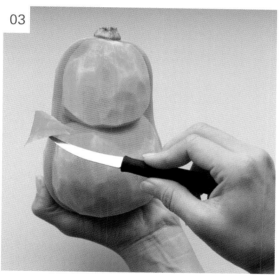

03

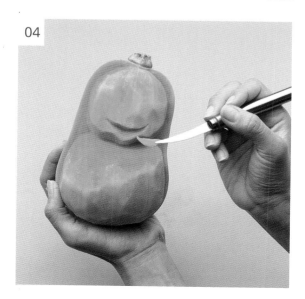

04

01. You will need a butternut squash, black radish, a piece of yellow beet, and some chives for this carving.

02. Peel the front half of the squash about 3 mm deep with the **Thai knife**.

03. Cut out three wedges between the body and head with the **Thai knife**—one from the front and one each from the left and right sides. This makes a division between the head and body. Round off the wedge cuts with the **Thai knife**.

04. Cut the mouth out with the **Thai knife**. Holding the knife at a right angle to the squash, make a cut curving upward on both sides. Angle the knife upward to cut the lower lip. This will give the hedgehog a smile.

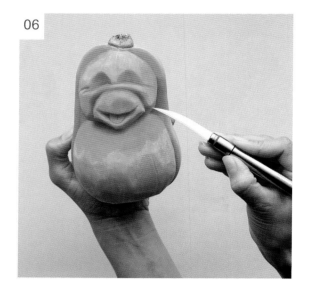

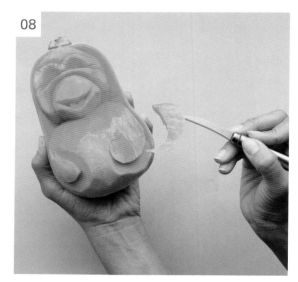

05. Cut the tongue in lightly and cut out the eye sockets.

06. Cut in the features of the face. To create a friendly expression, make sure the lines are rounded, finely cut, and not too straight.

07. With the small **V knife (E1)**, cut the eyebrows out.

08. Cut out the arms and hands with the **Thai knife**.

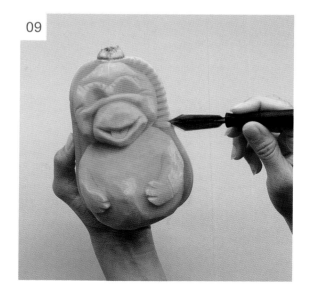

09. With the large **V knife (E3)**, cut the transition between the body and the quills.

10. Use the **V knife** to cut in the quills. Hold the **V knife** at an upward angle, cut about 1 cm deep, and bend the cutout quill slightly upward so that it stands out somewhat from the body.

11. Cut the eyes, ears, nose, bowtie, and feet out of the yellow beet and black radish. Glue the eyes on with vegetable adhesive and attach the larger pieces with toothpicks or adhesive. You can also put a small flower in one of the hedgehog's hands, use a style of your choice from chapter one. Attach the flower with a toothpick. Cover it with a piece of chive so the toothpick becomes a green stem.

12. The friendly hedgehog is finished. He will be a big hit, especially at a children's birthday party.

TIP

The seeds of the butternut squash are in the lower section. The upper half consists completely of nice firm pulp, which is ideal for carving.

10

11

12
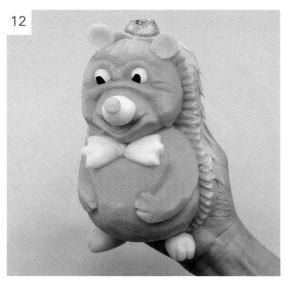

Squash Moon

Use a slice of butternut squash about 3 cm thick to make this half moon. A black radish works well for the eyes. The pattern on page 124 will help you with the general outline for this piece. The rest of the moon face is carved freehand. Keep the pattern beside you when you carve the facial features—this makes the work easier.

S

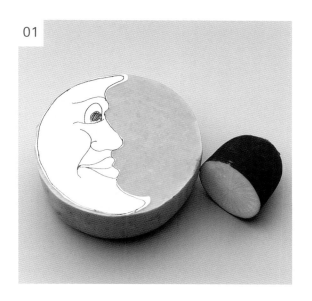

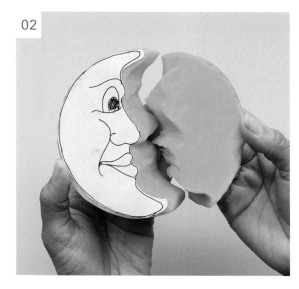

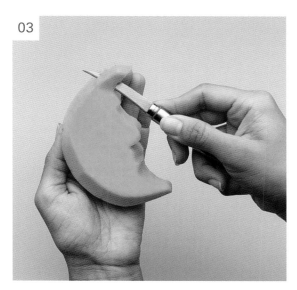

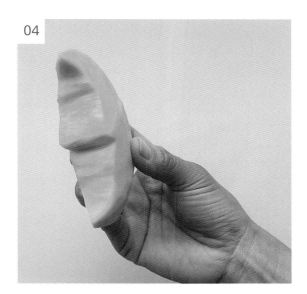

01. Copy the pattern, sized for the squash, and moisten it slightly so it sticks to the gourd.

02. Now cut out the outline with the **Thai knife** and remove the excess piece of squash.

03. Round the edges with the **Thai knife** to carve the basic shape of the moon.

04. A view of the moon from the front

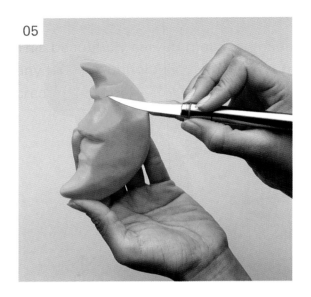

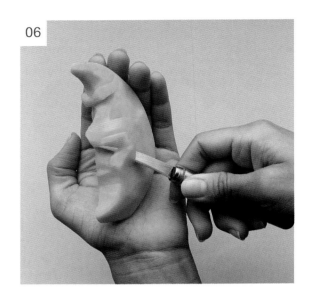

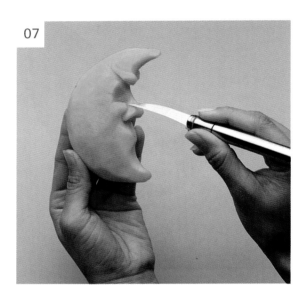

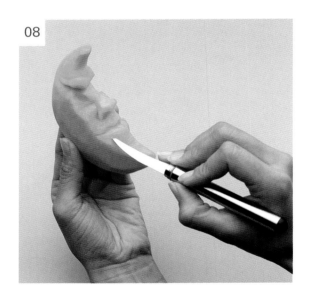

05. Cut out the eyebrows with the **Thai knife**.

06.-08. With the help of the pattern and the photos, carve the other facial features. Make sure that the face has rounded features so it does not seem too stiff.

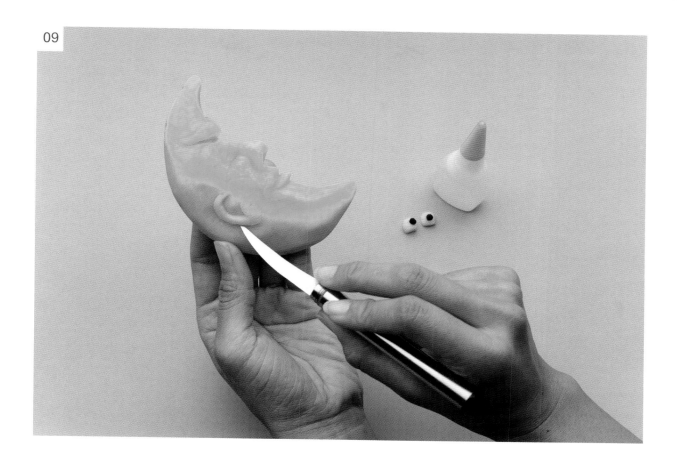

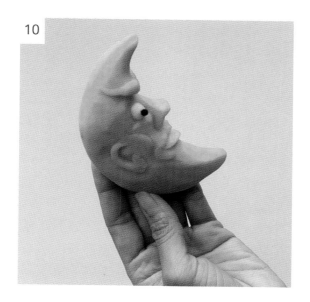

09. Finally, cut in the ears and then attach eyes made of the black radish using a short piece of toothpick or vegetable adhesive.

10. The finished moon provides a nice accent for your autumn decorations.

Christmas Melon

This Christmas decoration enchants with its fine workmanship and lovely color contrast, courtesy of the dark green melon rind. Naturally, you can use stars, angels, or other Christmas images instead of bells. Carve them into the melon and brighten up your holiday dinner with your own works of art.

E3   S

01

02

03

01. To make the bells symmetrical, use the pattern from page 123. Cut it out, moisten it slightly, and place it on the better looking, more even side of the melon.

02. Use the **Thai knife** to carve the outlines of the bells about 3 mm deep in the melon. Cut the rind away to reveal the bells and ribbons.

03. Cut the rind away in a circle around the bells.

TIP

With this technique you can carve a variety of images into the rind, including lettering, numbers, ornaments, animals, and more. There are no limits to your creativity!

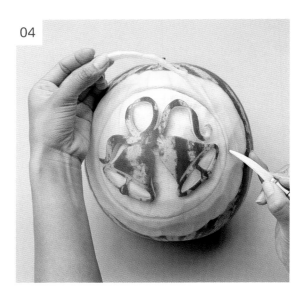

04. Cut a groove about 1 cm deep and 5 mm wide around the bells.

05. Now use the **V knife (E3)** to carve 2 cm long notches around the grooves. Direct the grooves toward the center of the melon and make sure they are spaced evenly.

06. Leave a border about 2 mm wide and start another row of notches. Make sure there are no gaps between notches.

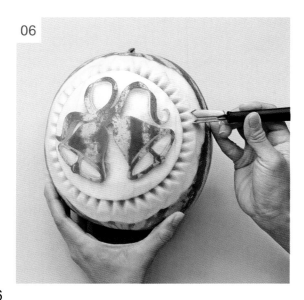

07. Repeat the last two steps for a second row of pointed flower petals.

08. To create a nice border, carve another row of notches around the outside with the **V knife (E3)**.

Little
Christmas Elf

This little Christmas elf goes well with cold winter days. Use a red beet for the hat to make a Santa Clause figure that will delight your children.

01

02

03

04

01. For the elf you need a black radish, a piece of carrot, a yellow beet, a piece of kohlrabi, and two peppercorns. Cut the radish into two parts so that the lower, thicker piece is about 10 cm long.

02. Use the **kerf knife** to cut the skin away in front for the face. The edges should look a bit uneven.

03. Cut out the two eye sockets with the **round knife (A4)**.

04. With the **ball shaper (012)**, cut the eyes out of the carrot piece and fasten the peppercorns to them as pupils. Carve the nose with the **ball shaper (020)**. Attach the eyes and nose with vegetable adhesive.

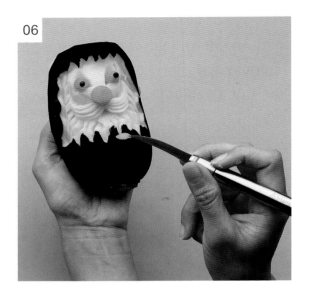

05. With the **Thai knife**, carve a moustache that curves upward. Then carve the beard with slightly curved lines.

06. Place a small piece of yellow beet for the mouth.

07./08. Use the beet to carve the hands and feet as well. They can be attached to the elf with toothpicks or vegetable adhesive.

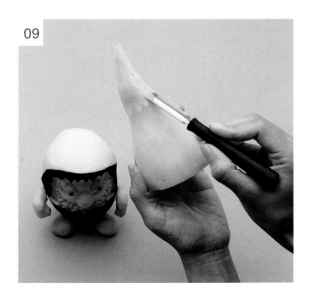

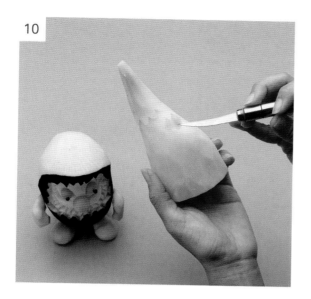

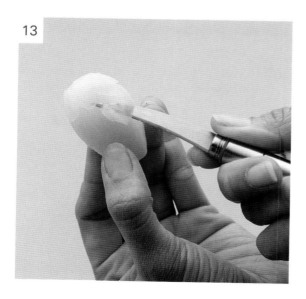

09. Peel the other half of the radish with a vegetable peeler. Use this piece to make the elf's hat. Make notches with the second smallest **round knife (A2)** about 3 mm deep all around.

10. With the **Thai knife**, cut the flesh away from below the scallops you just made, holding the knife at an angle, with the point upward. Repeat these two steps until the elf's hat is carved.

11. Attach the hat to the elf's head with a toothpick. Put the kohlrabi leaf in between. Attach a yellow vegetable pearl to the end of the hat with vegetable adhesive.

12./13. The elf still needs a fir twig to hold in his hand. For this, start with a piece of oval vegetable. Use the same technique as the hat for the twig. Then fasten the twig to the elf's hand with a toothpick.

The Snowflake

The carving technique you should use to make this beautiful snowflake is the same as the single-row flower (see page 21). Make these simple snowflakes in various sizes so you can use them as winter decorations for plates or even tree ornaments.

01. Use white vegetables like kohlrabi or radishes for the snowflakes.

02. Cut a slice about 1 cm thick out of the kohlrabi. Then cut eight notches at equal intervals with the **V knife (E2)**. These notches should not run all the way to the rind.

03. Cut in again behind the notches, far enough for the lines to meet. Do this by holding the knife at a greater angle to the vegetable slice.

04. Carve another row of notches that reach to the edge.

05./06. Make more notches to the left, right, and behind the last row of notches using the same angle as in step **03**.

07. Carefully break off the edge.

Carnival
in Venice

This mask is based on the classic Venetian carnival mask and can naturally be altered as you wish. If you would like, you can just use a few of the edible elements like the coils to create a nutritious decoration for a festive season.

Tools used, plus vegetable knife, vegetable adhesive, and toothpicks

A1   E1   S   012   N1-N2

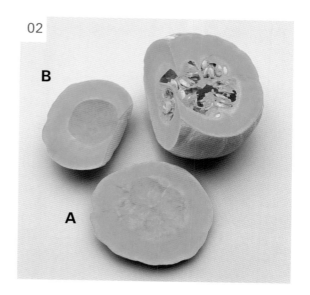

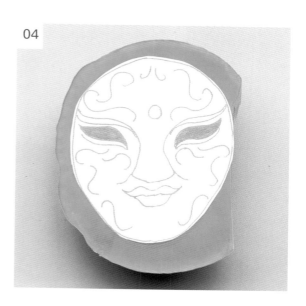

01. Make sure that your pumpkin has a relatively smooth surface and is not too strongly ribbed. If the ribs have to be cut away, the remaining pulp will be very thin.

02. With a **vegetable knife**, cut the underside off the pumpkin. This gives you the back of the mask (A). Then cut a 7-8 cm piece off one side of the pumpkin (B). This becomes the mask.

03. Use the pattern on page 124 for the mask.

04. Cut out the pattern and place it on the cut side of the pumpkin piece to achieve a symmetrical mask shape.

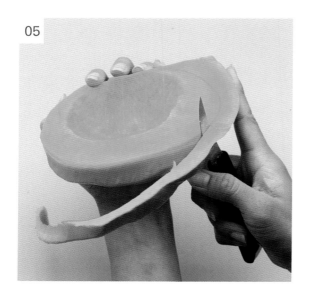

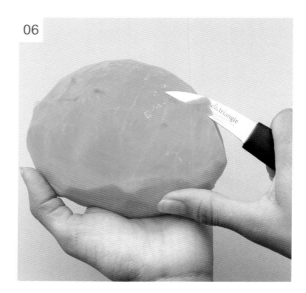

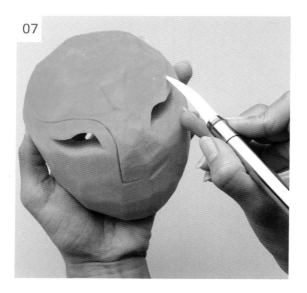

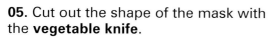

05. Cut out the shape of the mask with the **vegetable knife**.

06. Remove the rind on the front of the mask with the **vegetable knife**, leaving a relatively smooth surface.

07. With the **Thai knife**, cut out the eyes and then carve the lines of the eyebrows and the shape of the nose.

08. With the **Thai knife**, carve out the pumpkin under the eyebrows to about 1 cm deep. The eyebrows should be even with the nose.

09. Round the nose with the **Thai knife** and cut the midline of the mouth.

10. Cut out the mouth. For the upper lip, hold the **Thai knife** with the tip angled downward—for the lower lip, angle the knife upward. Make a groove with the small **round knife (A1)** from the upper lip to the middle of the nose.

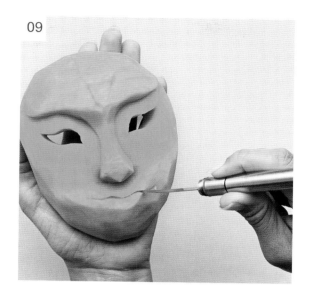

09

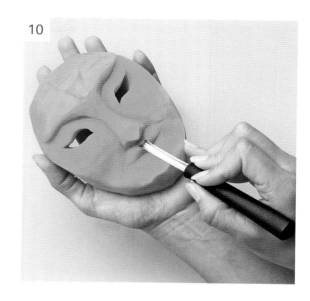

10

11

11. Cut some pulp away under the lower lip.

12. With the **Thai knife**, carve the upper line of the eyebrows and remove some of the pulp.

13. With the small **V knife (E1)**, cut lines around the eyes and additional lines along the mask according to your taste.

12

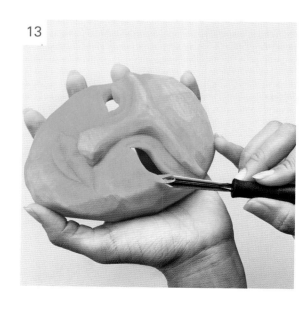

13

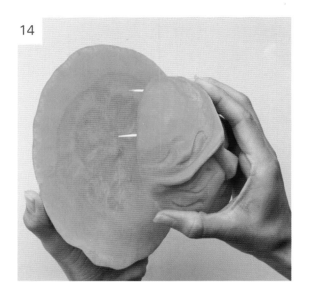

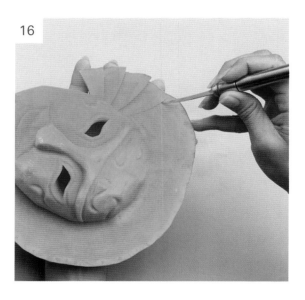

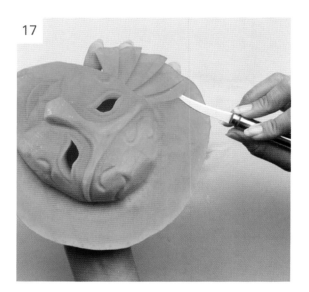

14./15. Attach the mask to the round slice of gourd with toothpicks.

16./17. Carve fanlike notches in the surface around the mask with the **Thai knife**.

18. Continue this pattern by cutting small pieces out from the outside.

19. Cut out various vegetable pearls with the **ball shaper (012)** and place them around the mask using vegetable adhesive or small pieces of toothpick. Be sure to place one pearl on the forehead of the mask.

20./21. Now you can decorate the mask. A few small flowers from chapter one are very suitable for this decoration. You can also add some vegetable coils, which can be carved out of vegetables with the **large and small potato spirals**.

TIP

For these more demanding decorations, always choose vegetables that are very firm so that you can carve clear, defined lines. If the fruit pulp is too thin, facial features like the nose can only be made flat, and with some difficulty. We recommend a fairly smooth Muscat pumpkin, which you can get at Carnival time. You can also use a large, round turnip.

19

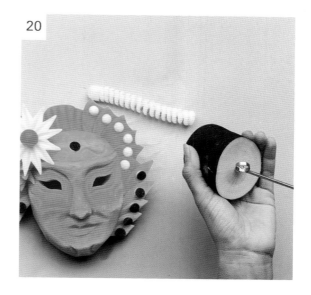

20

21

Fish 1

Fish 2

Bells

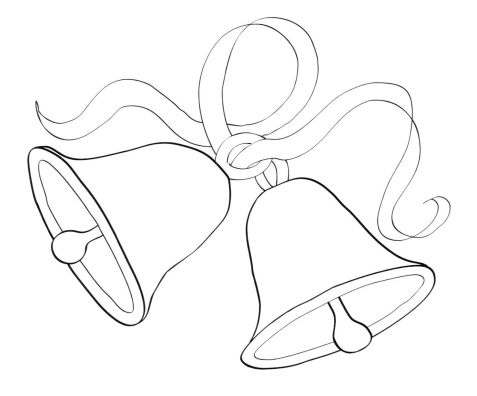

Sun

Moon

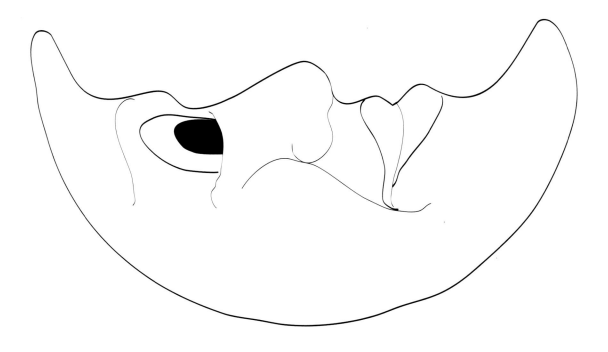

Mask

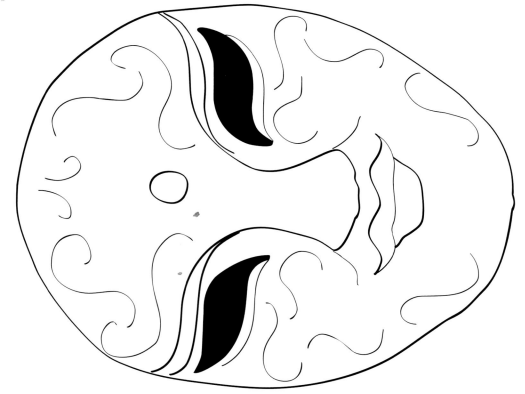

Witch

Resources

There is a wide variety of garnishing and carving tools available on the market for your carving needs. The set featured throughout this book is part of the Triangle brand, which is manufactured by Hill Metallwaren GmbH in Germany (http://www.triangle-tools.de).

The following company offers Triangle brand products in the United States:

Fante's Inc.
Philadelphia, PA
Tel:1-800-443-2683
http://www.fantes.com

Other fruit and vegetable carving tools are available through the following:

Chef Depot Inc.
Downer's Grove, IL
Tel: 1-630-739-5200
http://www.chefdepot.com

Chef Knives to Go
Madison, WI
Tel: 1-888-792-2094
http://www.chefknivestogo.com

CutleryAndMore.com
East Dundee, IL
Tel: 1-800-650-9866
http://www.cutleryandmore.com

Galasource Ventures
Denver, CO
Tel: 1-866-966-0111
http://www.galasource.com

International Culinary Consultants
Lakewood, NJ
Tel: 1-732-886-1444
http://www.chefharvey.com

Kerekes Bakery & Restaurant Equipment Inc.
Brooklyn, NY
Tel: 1-718-232-7044
http://www.bakedeco.com

Knife Merchant, LLC
San Diego, CA
Tel: 1-800-714-8226
http://www.knifemerchant.com

PastryItems.com
Bel Air, MD
Tel: 1-443-417-8854
http://www.chefknifes.com

Temple of Thai
Beaverton, OR
Tel: 1-877-811-8773
http://www.templeofthai.com

Veggy Art LLC
Chantilly, VA
Tel: 1-703-919-7819
http://www.veggyart.com

Other types of food decorating supplies are available through the following:

Lucks Food Decorating Company
Tacoma, WA
Tel: 1-800-426-9778
http://www.lucks.com

The Baker's Kitchen
Toledo, OH
Tel: 1-419-381-9693
http://www.thebakerskitchen.net

The following organizations offer fruit and vegetable carving classes. (Please contact these organizations before making travel plans to attend classes.):

Art Chef Inc.
Hayward, CA
Tel: 1-510-368-2509
http://www.artchef.com

The Carving Institute
Bangkok, Thailand
Tel: 66-(0)-86-013-7645
http://www.carvinginstitute.com

Chicago Carving Creations
Chicago, IL
Tel: 1-847-830-6858
http://www.chicagocarvingcreations.com

Veggy Art LLC
Chantilly, VA
Tel: 1-703-919-7819
http://www.veggyart.com

Other resources:

American Culinary Federation
St. Augustine, FL
1-800-624-9458
http://www.acfchefs.org

The American Institute of Wine and Food
Carmel, CA
1-800-274-2493
http://www.aiwf.org

Food Service Educators Network International
Chicago, IL
1-312-849-2220
http://www.feni.org

International Association of Culinary Professionals
Atlanta, GA
1-800-928-4227
http://www.iacp.com

National Association of Catering Executives
Columbia, MD
1-410-290-5410
http://www.nace.net

United States Personal Chef Association
Rio Rancho, NM
1-800-995-2138
http://www.uspca.com

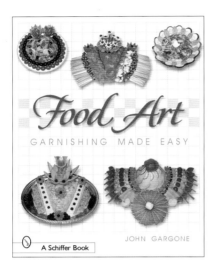

Food Art: Garnishing Made Easy. John Gargone. With over 370 color photos, John Gargone takes readers step-by-step through the process of creating garnishes that are stunning works of edible art. Follow the straight-forward, systematic instructions to create salad border garnishes, salad and table centerpieces, fruit displays ranging from bird cages to watermelon wedding vases, melon sculpture displays, masterpieces in cheese, vegetables, and deli spreads.

| Size: 8 1/2" x 11 | 371 color photos | 96 pp. |
| ISBN: 0-7643-1960-4 | soft cover | $19.95 |

Food Presentation: Tips & Inspiration. Michelle Valigursky. Food that looks beautiful does tastes better! Learn hundreds of tips and tricks that restaurant chefs rely on to wow their guests. Basic techniques and ordinary household items will become your tools in adding drama, interest, and impact to your food presentation.

| Size: 8 1/2" x 11" | 234 color photos | 128 pp. |
| ISBN: 978-0-7643-3481-8 | soft cover | $24.99 |

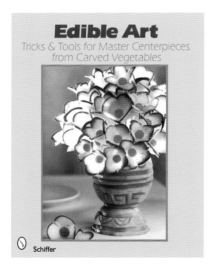

Edible Art : Tricks & Tools for Master Centerpieces. Edible Art . Simple techniques and tools make it possible to create absolutely stunning centerpieces that will be the talk of the party. Butterflies and rosebuds from colorful beets, carrots, and radishes are easily crafted. Elaborate melon lanterns and "flower" filled vases are crafted step-by-step in pictures, making it easy for you to follow the directions. Twenty-five splendid projects promise to delight dinner guests, and gratify their maker.

| Size: 8-1/2" x 11" | 305 color photos | 128 pp. |
| ISBN: 0-7643-2513-2 | soft cover | $19.95 |

Creating Floral Centerpieces. Bill Murphy. Professional floral designer Bill Murphy, AFID, takes you step-by-step through the creation of more than 25 impressive floral displays, from charger plates and napkin rings to kettle-sized, exotic centerpieces. From basic bouquet tying skills through the latest techniques using wire and floral adhesive, you will be inspired to adorn every event with flowery creations.

| Size: 8 1/2" x 11 | 288 color photos | 112 pp. |
| ISBN: 978-0-7643-3459-7 | hard cover | $29.99 |